MORE JOKES

NEW JOKES

FROM BARBADOS

BY
KEMMERICK "BING BONG" HARRISON

ISBN: 976-8215-43-7
ISBN: 978-976-8215-43-7

BY
KEMMERICK "BING BONG" HARRISON

PREFACE

Every day comedy reveals itself to us in several forms, but it usually goes unnoticed to the unsuspecting **ears or eyes.** When you are looking or listening for it, you see and hear it.

From things I observe, I have created these new jokes, which I have tried on a few close friends and family to ensure acceptability.

The jokes were refined where necessary, to ensure that the material is not perceived as rude, lewd or crude.

One can never guarantee that everyone will take the jokes in the spirit of humour. In fact I find, people will not try to create a single joke but will pick to pieces some of mine, at times reading into them what was never intended. Let me reinforce the point therefore that it is not my intention to offend anybody. This book is geared towards adults. Parents with an open mind who allow their children to read this material will find that it encourages analytical thought that improves comprehension.

Sit back, relax and thank our Creator for instilling in me the ability to make people laugh. Laughter, as all of us know can be therapeutic.

Throughout the book I have requested that individuals respect my copyright interest. These jokes are not to be recorded for financial gain. Such action is strictly prohibited. All producers wishing to use any of my creative work please contact me for the necessary permission.

With Love
Kemmerick "Bing Bong" Harrison

Content

SILVER

A friend bought his newly found love two silver bracelets.

Feeling slightly disappointed, she asked him why silver and not gold.

He told her he had bought silver to match the colour of her hair.

She was a brunette with long black hair so she did not understand.

If he had bought her a bracelet made of hematite (a black stone) she said it would make more sense.

He turned to her and asked, "Is your head the only place that has hair?"

MIDGET

When Judge Benn entered the courtroom the court's Marshall called on everyone to stand.

The judge was about to take his seat, when he saw a man in the back of the courtroom still sitting.

Policemen were ordered to arrest the man. They claimed he was in contempt of court.

When they approached the gentleman to make the arrest the policemen began laughing. The man was a midget.

5

PLANTS

A child in a lesson on plants was taught how new plants were created.

The teacher explained that new plants were created when seeds or suckers (pieces of plants) are planted."

When his mother heard that trees were created from suckers she said to her son, "Looks like we will have to plant your Dad."

GET UP

Mavis worked all day cleaning the house and was very tired when she retired for the night.

In the middle of her sleep she kept hearing her husband repeating the words "Get up! Get up! Get up!"

Mavis thinking he was referring to her said , "I am tired; Please let me rest."

He said to her, "Woman! Can't I have a conversation with a part of my body?

CHRISTIAN

A young man met a Christian lady who took him to church. The priest told him that if he was truly in love and wanted to develop a lasting Christian relationship he needed to be born again.

The young man looked at the priest and said, "There is no way I am going back up into my mother."

PUPIL

A teacher in a spelling lesson called on the children in her class to spell "Things they would see in a classroom".

The first child was asked to spell table.

The next was asked to spell chair.

The teacher then called on the third child to spell pupil.

He asked, "Which pupil? Pupil as in student or pupil as in eye?"

MARRY ME

As John and Harriett chatted John found that he liked her personality. His affection for her gradually grew.

After a few hours of knowing her he asked her to marry him.

She quickly agreed to marry him. They set the date and decided on the church.

In his customized suit and neatly clad, he turned up at the church on the agreed day.

You would not believe this but the lady who agreed to marry him was the priest. She was waiting to conduct the ceremony.

OLYMPICS

After going to three consecutive Olympics and not winning a medal my school mate went to a local store and bought his own (a medal).

ABSTAIN

A group of ladies got together and decided to meet at a church to make a pledge to abstain until they were married.

In the front pew sat an old lady of seventy two, with a "T" Shirt which read:-

"CAN"T GET ..."

When she turned around the "T" Shirt read:-   "ENOUGH".

DELAYS

A young lady was delayed at the airport awaiting the arrival of her aircraft for more than five hours. A gentleman came up to her and asked, "Are you here, still waiting for your plane?"

Her reply was, "My friend, the plane is like my husband. He takes long to come."

A MAN

Good grammars dictates that we should always say it is, instead of it are. Similarly we should never say a men. Instead the correct grammar is a man. John the son of Martha kept saying I are, I are, I are repeatedly. It was so disgusting that his mother Martha asked him, "Son! Why don't you use the correct grammar?" He said to her, "But Mum, you are always using the wrong grammar too" She asked him, "What do you mean?" His reply was, "Mum! At night when you pray I always hear you say, Amen, a men, a men.

MAD

Two mad men were in conversation when one asked the other, "How did you know you were going mad? He said he knew he was going mad when he kept searching and looking for spectacles that he had on. The other said other people told him he was mad because he asked the judge who re-manded him to the *Mad House* if she was mad.

RISKY

A man met his best friend and because he did not see him for a very long time, asked him, "How is your love life?" His reply was, "Boy with all of these diseases around I don't take risk. I make a fist and use my wrist."

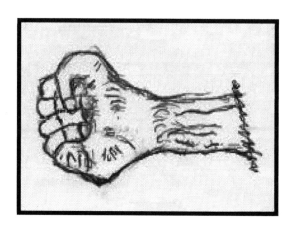

TRUST

John's mother left him in her corner store to sell ("bits and pieces") some small items she had.

The previous week she hardly got any sales so John said to her as she was about to leave, "Mother! I doubt I will make any sales."

His mother said to him "Look on the bright side; we must trust God."

He turned to her and said, "Sorry Mother, all sales cash *I am not trusting Anybody.*"

10

RIDICULOUS

Some cops cannot and do not distinguish between the letter of the law and the spirit of the law.

Had this policeman who would report (give a ticket) every driver parked in a **NO PARKING AREA** at the airport even at times when it was not busy or when that vehicle was the only one parked.

It got so overbearing that people complained to some Senior Officers. The cop was eventually transferred to another location where he was now assigned to patrolling a major hospital. The cop was so ridiculous he reported his father for sneezing in a **SILENT ZONE.**

SERVICE

Instead of collecting him and bringing him to the church for the Sunday morning church service, she gave him the name of the street with directions to get there.

She kept looking for him as the preacher preached but never saw him. It was only after she left the church and was on her way home that she saw him. He sat well dressed with a bible in hand by the petrol station under the sign marked "**SERVICE AREA**".

FIREARM

After several attacks on cab drivers the Taxi Association had a meeting with the Commissioner of Police.

The chief of Police agreed that all taxi drivers would be given permission to have a licensed gun.

Everybody started applying to be a taxi driver.

BOASTFUL

A boastful young man kept telling his friends that while on a world tour he was intimate with seven women of six different nationalities.

I asked him , "How could that be possible when they would have all been speaking a different language?"

He said, "They all knew one language"

And what was that?" I asked.

He said, "Money!"

BURIED

A man told his children he did not want to die poor.

He instructed them, to withdraw all his money off his two bank account and put it in the coffin next to him.

When he died and his daughter went to withdraw his money, the total for his two accounts was one hundred and fifty three dollars and twenty-three cents.

12

PILOT

A man rushed into a Travel Agency and asked the agent on duty, "Do you fly to Caracas?"

The lady looked him in the face and asked, "Do I look like a pilot?"

FISH AND CHIPS

Robert went to a popular restaurant stole some "Fish and Chips", ate it, and refused to pay for it.

When arrested by the police and he told them that it was his mother who cooked it so he did not see why he should have to pay for it.

HURRICANES

After hurricane Katrina had devastated Louisiana everyone used all types of transportation to get out of Houston when they heard that hurricane Rita was heading in their direction. Some vehicles ran out of gas and people were stuck along the highway.

After Rita passed an old lady said on television that she travelled for five hundred (500) miles without having to buy gas.

The interviewer asked her how she was able to travel such a distance without having to buy gas.

She said she did not buy gas it was her husband who bought it.

AVIAN FLU

John decided to grow his own chicks because of Avian Flu (Bird Flu).

On morning John got up quite angry and filed for divorce simply because his wife told him, "Sorry sweetheart but I am no longer eating your bird."

PENS

A boy dropped off twenty unique looking pens at a village shop to be sold. In the evening when he returned he saw one pen on the sales stand so he turned to the sales clerk saying, "I see you have sold nineteen of the pens."

She said, "Well if one left, isn't it obvious that nineteen are sold?"

He said, "No because I thief one."

BIRD FLU

Because of the great fear of a Bird Flu epidemic customs officers at the air and sea ports had everyone under close surveillance.

In fact persons who were suspected of hiding birds to bring them into the country were asked to undress.

One man said that only a doctor can make him show his bird.

Another said that his bird is already dead and therefore cannot cause problems for anyone.

A woman in the queue reaction was "No one is searching me because do not have a bird."

She said she only had a cat.

You should have seen other men in that room; big birds, small birds half dead birds and some not so good looking birds.

Men with sick birds were detained.

N.B:- *In the Caribbean some parts of a person's body are named after animals.*

STRONG

Old people hardly ever get the best care in these homes for the aged.

My aunt came to visit my grand-dad in one of these homes. She said to him, "Man you looking strong."

All he could say was, "I not only look strong but I smell strong too." (of urine)

BONES

At the lunch and breakfast table Mark would hear his mother say, "Save the bones for the dog."

It was like the golden rule - Save the bones for the dog.

One evening his sister went missing and Mark went, "I hope the dogs didn't eat my sister."

ON CRICKET

Who was the fastest bowler that ever lived?

He was a one foot man named Foottie.

Someone would run up and give him the ball.

MOUNTAINS

After the tsunami in Asia a new island was formed in the Caribbean east of Barbados.

The land was made up of two mountains named Mt. Misery and Mt. Pleasant.

All the men lived on Mt. Pleasant.

16

HONEYMOON

A man and his wife to be, were planning their wedding when he turned to her and asked, "Sweetheart! Where will we be spending our honeymoon?"
She asked, "What's the point of a honeymoon, when all of the honey has gone already?"

WELL

Impressed by a well digger's ability to shape and dig wells with such speed his employer asked him what made him pursue such a career.
He said, "From the time he was a child his mother always told him to go to school and learn well."

RANGE

A man went into a public bathroom, closed the door, sat on the toilet and began to ease his bowels.
It was indeed a strange bowel movement, for all you were hearing was pax, pax, padax, pax.
The noise became so overbearing the a youngster in the bathroom shouted, "Skipper! Is in there a shooting range?"

CHANGE IT

A young man called a hardware store and asked that a special toilet bowl be made (customize) for him.

He asked that it be made taller and deeper.

He said that he made such a request because whenever his uncle sat on the toilet the tip of his "stick" took a dip.

CAR RENTAL

In Miami car rental companies go by names that entice customers to rent their vehicles. There is Budget Rentals, Dollar Rentals and companies with all sorts of enticing names.

Thomas' father came home one evening and announced, "I have booked a family trip to Miami. We will be staying at the Newport Beach Hotel and I have reserved a Dollar car.

His seven year old son shouted, "A dollar car Dad?" Pulling out a dollar he said, "In that case I'll pay for the car."

CAT OR RAT

A boy was told he would have to spend his summer vacation with his grandmother.

All was well until he was told that his grandmother had cataract.

He refused to go saying, "Sorry! I don't mind cats but I hate rats"

18

WOW WOW

A man became engrossed in a game of Scrabble at a Chinese restaurant. He asked the waiter to bring him something to eat.

Well all the chicken and fried rice was gone so the waiter brouhgt him what he had.

He ate and played ate and played but only realised what he was fed when the waiter passed and asked, "How was the Bow Wow?".

MINI BUS DIPLOMA

Mini Bus drivers got together recently and opened a college offering a diploma in driving.

Courses offered were:

1. Overtaking Dangerously
2. Overloading
3. Exceeding Speed Limits
4. Disregard for Law and Order

These courses were offered for the first semester. Unfortunately however the diploma was put on hold because the primary instructor a driver was sentenced to eight years in prison for causing the death of ten persons due to reckless driving.

19

GOLD TOOTH

My cousin kept boasting and showing off her gold rings, gold chains and a customized gold tooth to her friends. She said how she had loved her boyfriend so much because he would always buy her jewellery for her birthday or at Christmas time.

One day I saw her with the tooth missing, Quite surprised I asked her, "What happened?"

She said that she and her boyfriend had fallen out (broken off the relationship) and the first thing he took back was her gold tooth.

BEST MAN

At a recent wedding the bridegroom got so inebriated (drunk) at the reception that he was unable to stick the cake.

Guess who came forward to do it.

The bestman because he said he was the bestman so he was the best man to stick it.

He then turned to the wife and asked, "Do you think he will be sober for the honeymoon?"

SKELETONS

Two skeletons went into a restaurant. The waiter asked them to place their order. One ordered skin and the other bones.

20

DOGGIE BAG

Have you ever gone to a restaurant and because the food served was too much you had to order a Doggie Bag.

It happened to Kerry and I.

When we ordered a doggie bag the stupid waiter brought two condoms.

TELEPHONE BILL

His mother always sent him to pay the telephone bill and for three straight months he was asked to pay $289.27.

It was not a fixed rate telephone so to his mother it seemed strange.

She went to the office with her bills to question the payments.

When they checked the cashier was billing him for what was really her telephone number 28927.

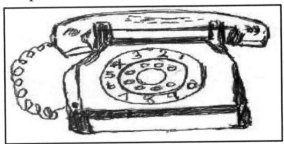

All she said was, "It is a good thing the number wasn't seven digit number.

RAP

A guy ran into a CD store, asking for a Rap CD meaning a CD of Rap music. The attendant wrapped a Reggae CD and gave him.

21

STOP

Mary decided to bake a cake but forgot to get the eggs. She told her husband to get into his car, rush down to the supermarket, buy the eggs and bring them back as soon as possible.

Two hours later he had not returned, so she jumped into her car to go and check to see what had happened.

There her husband was at the Major Stop where the sign read "STOP".

He said he was waiting for the sign to say "GO".

UNBELIEVABLE

In Barbados Pudding and Souse is a delicacy that the majority of nationals look forward to having on Saturday. There was always some discussion as to who made theirs the best.

Everyone in the neighbourhood where I lived, boasted that Shiela my next door neighbour made the best Pudding and Souse.

Everywhere you go the talk was no one could beat Sheila's Pudding and Souse. One day the secret got out.

Two fellows saw Sheila collecting the Pudding and Souse from someone living in another district.

All Sheila did was buy the Pudding and Souse from another lady and sell it.

FOOD

At a popular restaurant, management never restricted the workers from eating food in the kitchen.

They could eat whatever they wanted but were not allowed to bring anything out of the kitchen.

Some would eat so much that their stomachs bulged.

One evening after working hours when the staff was leaving the security guard decided to do a thorough search.

Realizing that the guard was searching not only bags but a worker's entire body, Ruth ran into the bathroom and removed six pounds of chicken and four loaves of bread she had strapped to her stomach.

When she came out to be checked the guard said, "I thought you were pregnant."

Her reply was, " I just lost the baby."

BAD BREATH

Mark came up to Vincent complaining that whenever he is in conversation with anyone, that person always turn his/her face and walk away from in front of him.

Vincent told him he should try speaking with his mouth closed.

EXERCISE

Every morning before sunrise people met at the Miami Beach to exercise. You should see them up and down the beach jogging and walking. However there were these two ladies who came but would be seen talking for hours instead of walking or running.

Every morning that was all they would do, chat, chat, chat; talk, talk and talk. One morning a bold faced man went up to them saying, "I thought you were here to exercise?"

Their reply was, "Can't you see we are exercising our mouths?"

WEDDING

There was a rehearsal for the wedding and the groom was told what he should say when the priest asked, "Do you take this woman to be your lawful wedded wife?"

On the evening of the wedding the priest read, "If anyone knows of any reason why these two should not be joined in holy matrimony, speak now or forever hold your peace."

The excitement had the groom so confused, he said, "I do!"

24

JAPANESE

A French couple and a Spanish couple invited their taxi driver out to dinner. Everyone knew English but the French couple had a conversation going in French while the Spanish couple spoke to each other in Spanish.

Now because the cab driver did not know French or Spanish he felt left out and got very annoyed. He said to them, "I bet you don't know that I speak Japanese."

They both said, "In that case teach us some Japanese words.

He went, "Panasonic, Sony, Toyota ..."

QUICK THINKER

A highly respected Sunday School teacher went to a village pharmacy and called for a pack of condoms.

To her surprise her neighbour was the cashier.

She exclaimed, "You know something I forgot to ask my brother what colour!"

ARMS MISSING

Big headlines in the newspaper read "POLICE ARMS MISSING."

A convict not understanding that guns and ammunition were what was missing said, "They should have taken their feet also."

25

CREAM

Mac was so naughty and nasty that he never liked to bathe. As a result his feet were white and scruffy.

His grandmother got tired of seeing his feet as white as chalk so she gave him some money and told him to buy some cream.

The boy bought ice-cream.

MISTAKEN

A young lady was walking the beach with her dad when she saw the physique of a muscular gentleman walking in front of them.

He overheard the young lady saying, "Oh what a muscular man with muscles well toned. He is so cute and very handsome.

On hearing this the gentleman turned around smiling.

When she saw his face she said, "I was speaking about my father."

26

CRAFTY

John was in love with Mavis for years. Despite his pleadings she never once gave him a chance to be that special person in her life.

One day to his surprise Mavis called him on the telephone and told him to come over because she wanted him to eat her.

In a few minutes he was at her door.

He sat down at the table. She offered him a rum and coke. She then uncovered a sculpture of herself she made out of bread and told him to eat. You would not believe the part of her he ate first.

BASEMENT

My grandfather was a man who enjoyed life. He never spent money on repairing his house. Instead he spent his money on rum, ladies and the good life.

His house was left in a state of disrepair and the wood which made the floor was old and weak.

One evening he came home, unlocked the door and as he stepped in through the door he fell through the floor.

His son who heard the commotion shouted, "Dad! Where are you?"

His reply was, "Relaxing in the basement."

JACUZZI

I never knew that mothers in the Caribbean referred to a girl's reproductive organ as a cat and a boy's as a dog until I went to visit my aunt. My aunt sent her daughter to bathe and told her not to forget to bathe her cat. When she came out of the bathroom the first question she asked was, "Did you bathe your cat?"

That evening her mother filled up the Jacuzzi with water and told the child she was going to let the water massage her tired body.

When she stepped into the water to lie down , the daughter shouted, "Mother! Careful you don't drown your cat."

Just as her mother came out of the Jacuzzi the little girl's brother jumped in saying, "It's a long time now; my dog has been starving, I think it is better if I drown him."

LIVES

I took my aunt's little girl for a stroll.
The little girl kept walking in the street instead of on the pavement. She got very angry when I kept insisting that she walked on the pavement.
She turned to me saying how she had ten lives.
It was only when she explained that I understood.
She said she had ten lives because she had one life and her cat had ten.

COMA

Roger went to the family doctor for an AIDS test. He heard that the lady he was dating had a boyfriend who had died of the disease.
Roger was so scared he was trembling from teeth to toe.
Five days after his blood was taken the doctor called him in for the results.
Roger sat down. The doctor opened his file (folder).
Roger looked over his shoulder and saw positive.
He fainted the same time.
When he came out of the coma, the doctor told him that the results he saw really belonged to someone else.
Roger was all right.

MONEY IS NOT MY PRIMARY AIM, BUT WHEN YOU EMAIL MY J OKES Y OU L EAVE M E WITH NOTHING TO GAIN. REFRAIN: NO EMAIL PLEASE!

OVERSIZED

She was pure and untouched, still she became pregnant.

How could this be?

Then she remembered.

She had gone to the doctor. He sedated her (put her to sleep).

Then she remembered asking, "Doc isn't that needle is much bigger than the normal size?"

CHEATING

"My husband is honest and faithful, never cheating on me!" Mary boasted.

One day she challenged him to test his honesty.

She knew that she would never ever have a relationship with anyone one but him, but to test him she proposed that they both cheat on each other, at least once.

"I want to see how it feels," she told him.

A coin would be tossed and the winner would start the ball rolling (first to cheat).

The toss was spun and the husband won.

Feeling sure that he would say he couldn't do it, she got a big surprise.

He told her it was her turn because he had cheated already.

CASINO

Joe followed his workmates and went to the Casino. He lost all his monthly wages.

He went home and told his wife, "Honey I will not be able to give you any money to pay the bill this month because I lost the money in the Casino." Thinking that she might be angry he was shocked when she said, "Well! Get a bath, change your clothes and let us go to look for it.

TAKE OFF

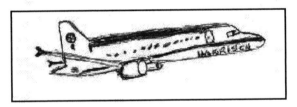

Her nineteen-year old son had just gotten his licence.

Against her will she lent him her new car.

In less than fifteen minutes he was calling her telling her the car was written off (damaged beyond repair). It had knocked down a series of signs and stop signals in close proximity to the National Airport.

She said, "But I told you not drive fast."
He said, "Mother! When I saw the aeroplanes I just felt like I could take off.

DYING

Jack and Sharee arranged to meet in Barbados to spend the Easter weekend so he called Sharee saying I and dying to be with you.

She got mad with him telling him to cut it out because if he dies he would be of no help to her.

MAKING LOVE

Mavis heard friends say how Tim was cheating on her. Whenever she confronted him his answer was he did not cheat.

One Sunday they made love all day. He then put on his clothes to go home. Meaning to ask him if he had made love to someone else other than her she asked him, "When was the last time you made love?"

Tim did not get a chance to answer.

Mavis' son who is always eavesdropping shouted, "Mother it would have to be just now, with you."

AMBASSADOR

An Olympian was given the title "AMBASSADOR" on returning home with a medal.

A few years later he kept complaining that he was not getting the respect he deserved.

He only understood the true meaning of the title when a little boy said, "Ambassador has *ass* in it."

MARRIAGE

Carmen a blind lady visited the Caribbean and was swept off her feet by a sweet black Bajan man.

She told one of her friends that the guy was so sweet she was sure he was struck with a sugar stick.

Her friend asked her, "But how did you know he was black."

She said, "By the size of his broomstick."

CRICKET

At a beginner's class for the game of cricket everyone was asked to bring a bat, a ball and two pads.

Jonathan's father gave him the bat. His uncle gave him some balls.

For pads he sneeked into his sister's room and took two of hers

SHOCKING

An old man bought a cell. phone from a store and brought it back the next day. He complained that the phone was shocking him.

The attendant then called his cell. number. He dropped the phone saying, "See what I tell you! It is shocking me"

She took up the phone and checked. It was on vibrate.

MISUNDERSTANDING

Maria live in the countryside where in those days there were hardly any paved roads, electricity and telephones.

On day she went to visit her uncle. The telephone rang and Maria's uncle shouted, "Maria the telephone is for you!"

Maria went unplugged the telephone and put it in her bag.

IMPRESSIVE

She was spelled bound. He came and he offered an all expensive paid trip to one of her favourite islands.

The mistake he made was when he said he would do the spending.

He did not mind buying the outfit, shoes and bags but he started to ball when they reached the airport. In the duty free she wanted the most expensive perfumes and liquor.

It was when she called on him to buy an expensive bracelet that he called off the trip.

BIG BUCKS

A ninety six year old man with six children, fourteen grands and twenty great grands won the State Lottery.

Instead of taking a lump sum payment he opted to take the money in instalments over a twenty year period. He died the next week.

FLYING FISH

A tourist visiting the island of Barbados bought some flying fish cooked and wrapped in foil. He refused to remove the foil.

He was thinking it might fly away.

COMMON TREND

Jack's son liked aeroplanes so he became a pilot. His daughter was in training to be an astronaut.

Jack himself always seized the opportunity to be flying from state to state or island to island.

In an interview, Jack's mother was asked why her children and grand children always seem to like flying.

She said from the time they were small she fed them flying fish, flying fish; flying fish."

TRUTHFUL

An attractive lady was reading my joke book and just would not stop laughing.

I turned to her and asked, "Are you enjoying it?"

Her reply was, "It is so sweet"

Smiling I said, "That is exactly what my sweetheart told me last night when I asked her that same question."

She said I wish I could say the same for my little Pigtail.

DANDRUFF

My best friend came to me one day saying he had met the darling of his life.

He talked of the things she did to make him happy.

He said he had a dandruff problem and this young lady would get a comb and scratch his hair to remove the dandruff. She was so gentle that he would often fall asleep.

She often gave him a little nudge saying, "Wake up, stop falling asleep on me"

He said he would open his eyes with a smile thinking that he never knew one woman could be so sweet.

A year later I met him and he told me that he got married . Now from the things he told me I do not think I want to get married.

Starting with the dandruff problem he said to me that he had to stop her scratching his hair because right after he put the ring on her finger her hand like it got too heavy. Instead of a soft gentle scratch the digging got so rough that the hair started to drop out.

From what I could see he was beginning to go bald. His going to sleep ceased when she scratched it.

He went on and on.

ELTON AND JOHN

Elton saw John sitting on a chair and said to him, "I want what you are sitting on."

He got up and gave him the chair.

He turned to him and say, "I probably was not clear but you know I don't mean the chair."

WARNING

I went to a bar and saw a young man crying. In front of him the sign read *"The Minister of Health reminds you that smoking is dangerous to your health"*.

He said that his father had died of lung cancer.

Feeling sorry for him I asked, "Who is your father?"

He said, "The Minister of Health".

PINA COLADA

A friend, my sweetheart and I decided to order some drinks at a local bar.

She ordered a Pina Colada while I ordered a Virgin Pina Colada.

I asked my friend if he too wanted a Virgin Pina Colada.

His answer was, "Leave out the Pina and Colada. Just bring the Virgin.

BARBADOS

In Barbados the names of places fascinate me. Mount Hillaby the highest mountain is nothing more than a hill. Penny Hole is still referred to as Penny Hole despite the name change to Gemswick a number of years ago.

Well! A British tourist was on a sight seeing tour of the island. She was dressed in a T Shirt with the map of Barbados printed at the front. She went up to this crazy guy asking him where she could find Mount Hillaby.

He took a good look at the map she wore. He shouted right there reaching out and touching her with his index finger on the tip of her breast.

She was angry but got the message.

Another fellow next to he said , "It was a good thing she didn't want me to show her Penny Hole."

BURNS

The ambulance came and took him to the hospital with first degree burns.

This is what happened.

He was hungry so he lit the stove. He put two hotdogs in the pan to fry them. He saw a container labelled Kerosene Oil and poured it into the pan.

N.B: *Kerosene oil is used as fuel for stoves especially in homes of the poor.*

STAMMERING GRANNY

My girlfriend's granny used to stammer so the wayu she would say things would make me laugh.

One day we dressed granny to take her out for an evening ride. Just as we were about to leave the house granny declared, I-I- I want to-to do-do-do something in the toilet.

We knew she was suffering with a slight case of diarrhoea so we sat outside to wait for her.

After waiting for about five minutes I went over to the bathroom and asked, "Granny! Are you ready yet?"

In an angry voice she shouted, " I-I-I ain't fin-- finish sh--sh -- sh it."

HORN

Never take a man seriously when he says that he can take a horn.

Tony boasted that he could take a horn until his wife to be, cheated on him and he found out.

He cried like a baby. He couldn't get his favourite food to go down.

Things got so bad that one day while watching the television he heard the telephone ringing. He saw it was the telephone in the television, still he ran picked up the television, put it to his ear to answer the phone.

SEXY

It was his teacher's birthday so Tony presented her with strawberries, eggs, Xora (flowers) and some yams.

When she hugged him and kissed him on the cheek, he said to her, "Spell out the name of each gift then write down the beginning letter of each present in the order in which I presented them and you will see what I have been thinking of your for years."

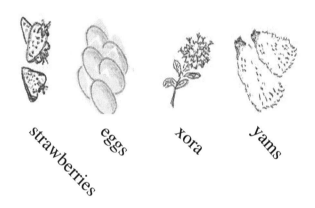

strawberries   eggs   xora   yams

SHOPLIFTERS

The sign read:

"SHOPLIFTERS WILL BE PROSECUTED"
A young lady brought it to my attention saying, "The owner would have to be stupid to think that someone would attempt to lift up a shop made of concrete."

TUCKS

Two neighbours were jealous of each other, always arguing about who was prettier.

The younger one took some pictures, put them in a book and called the book "Sweet and Sexy"

Quite jealous of her the elder lady decided to do a book also.

She mounted the pictures in the book, showed them to her husband and asked him to suggest a name for the book.

Without thinking of the consequences he said, "Tucks and Wrinkles"

LAST NIGHT

A lady read a joke in one of my joke books and laughed out loudly.

I asked her, "Was it good?"

Her reply was, "That was so sweet!"

I look her in the face and said, "That is what my sweetheart said to me last night when I asked her the same question."

With a sad look on her face she said, "Unfortunately I can't say the same thing for my partner Pigtail if he were to ask me that question."

MONEY IS NOT MY PRIMARY AIM, BUT WHEN YOU EMAIL MY JOKES YOU LEAVE ME WITH NOTHING TO GAIN. REFRAIN: NO EMAIL PLEASE!

POISONOUS

Jack and his sister Jill refused to return home one afternoon after school. Instead they opted to go by their grandmother.

They asked, "Grandma! Can we stay with you? Mummy wants to poison us."

Grandma called the mother right away.

The mother said that she was speaking to her friend on the phone about the snakes spotted in the neighbourhood and she was saying that they were poisonous.

HORNS

A man left home in a hurry for work. He was about two miles away from home when he remembered that he had left the stove on baking a chicken.

He took out his cellular phone and called back home.

Another man answered the telephone.

As you know man cant take horn so he turned around the vehicle and in a hurry he was back at home.

He saw his wife in the garden and went to her accusing her of bringing another man into his house.

When he finished, she simply told him she had forgotten to tell him she had put in a new answering machine.

ME TOO

A traveller who was uncertain about the boarding gate for Virgin Atlantic flight out Barbados went to a young lady standing in queue asking her, "Are you Virgin?'

When she said yes, her friend standing in front of her said, "Me too!"

CAMOUFLAGE

Aunt Susie remained hidden indoors because people called her fat. Fed up of hiding she went to a gym to register for an exercise programme. A computer generated voice would announce payment based on weight.

The normal fee was about two to two hundred and fifty dollars per person.

When my aunt got on the scale the computer generated voice said, "One thousand five hundred dollars please."

DEATH IN THE FAMILY

Johnny sat quietly in a corner of the classroom sobbing.

As he wept the teacher came over to find out what was the matter.

Johnny told her there was death in the family. He said Mummy told him his Daddy is dead.

The teacher a family friend dialled his house to express her sympathy.

Johnny's mother told the teacher not to worry since it was her way of telling Johnny that Daddy was impotent.

SCORE

They watched cricket together. He knew the game but she did not.

When the commentator said the score was two for sixty-nine, she said, "Let's go to bed."

Another wicket fell on the same score.

The maid knocked on the door asking "Can it be, "Three for sixty nine?"

EXCESSIVE

An old man wanted Kay to accompany him to his friend's wedding so she told him he had to outfit her.

Two days later she said she had shopped around and saw an outfit complete with bag, shoes and dress at a cost of $1200.00.

He could hardly afford the money but he squeezed it out of his pension cheques and gave her.

He was proud to have her next to him at the wedding.

You should have seen eyes popping out of heads.

They were telling him how sexy his "young ting" looked.

He really enjoyed himself and was telling friends he met that she made him feel like sweet sixteen again.

The next day he got a shock. By sheer coincidence he caught her returning the outfit at a rental shop.

44

THEFT

A young man was charged with the theft of a DVD.

On the day of his trial the judge asked him to give a good reason why he should not be sent to prison.

He produced a clipping from the front page of the local newspaper and said to the judge, "Sir the charges should never have been brought in the first place because as I entered the house I saw a DVD player in the living room and sitting next to it was this newspaper with FREE DVD'S written on it.

SMALL PIECE

Denise baked a cake and offered her neighbour John a piece. He loved the cake so much he told her that she must leave him a piece the next time she baked.

Two months later she baked a huge fruit cake. She cut out a small piece, wrapped it and left it on the table next to remainder of the cake. When John came to collect the cake Denise was on the toilet so she told him to take the piece of cake on the table.

Stupid John took up the bigger piece.

CAUGHT

Johnny swore he never cheated on his wife until she caught him 'red handed'.

He went by his outside woman and after a night of fun he fell off to sleep.

He got up in a rush to hurry home and in the dark he put the outside woman's underwear by mistake.

STUPID

A rookie policeman earned the nickname "The Major Stop policeman."

All he did was report people at the airport for not making a complete stop at this Major Stop.

He was so ridiculous that at home his mother came out of her bedroom, bumped into him and he reported her because she didn't stop.

SORRY

He stabbed him and he died.

His lawyer asked him to say he was sorry as this would help to reduce the number of years he would spend behind bars.

Well! You know these young people. He did not want to say sorry until his mother convinced him.

He then began, "Sir I am sorry, I am very sorry it was a broken bottle I used, it should have been my gun instead."

SNAKES

The government department responsible for catching snakes asked persons seeing snakes to call the SNAKE HOT LINE, should there be a sighting of any snake.

My cousin called to report the sighting of a snake.

He reported it as being the living room of his house.

When the officers came to catch the snake they were surprised and shock. His naked, drunk dad was lying on the floor.

All one of the officers could say was, "It could pass for a lizard but certainly not a snake.

NEW MATHS

A teacher could not understand why one of his students constantly said one and one made five $(1 + 1 = 5)$ until he explained.

He said, "When my mother and my father came together $(1+1)$ they made my sister and I and now my sister pregnant." $(1+1=5)$

47

BANK ROBBERY

A masked gunman robbed a bank and made off with thousands of dollars.

Quite shaken and nervous the teller ran over to the nearest police station to report the robbery.

She fainted in the police station because the stupid police officer forgot to take off the mask.

HALF BROTHER

A boy was introduced to his sister. The father said, "Son meet your half sister." He looked at his dad and asked, "Which half?"

LOVERS

Hazel's parents did not approved of her relationship with her newly found lover. He was just a mechanic and not a doctor or lawyer.

One evening her parent's car broke down and they called on her lover to repair what was a transmission problem.

He repaired the vehicle. Where the reverse should have been he put the drive and where the drive should have been he put the reverse.

When Hazel's dad got into the car to drive to church that evening, and it rammed into the back of the garage, all he said was, "That boy has got to go!"

FOR SALE

A young man from a rich family bought two new cars, a Mercedes Benz and a B.M.W.

You should have seen the number of young ladies who showed interest in him.

It took him one week before he fell in love with one of them.

Two weeks later he was advertising his cars for sale.

His mother could not understand why he was selling the new cars he had just bought so she asked him why.

This is what he told her, "Mother I no longer need a car because I have met Susan and she has two big bus."

NB: In the Caribbean the breast is referred to as bus.
I was unable to draw a picture of her bus because the size of the page would not be enough to hold them.

OUT

A guy was explaining the game of cricket to an American tourist. He said there are four different ways a batter can be out.

"There is stumped, bowled, caught and run out.", he said

A boy shouted, "You forget 'Thief Out'.

NOTES

Some school boys decided to make fast money.

One boy added a zero (0) behind the number 20 on the US twenty dollar note. The other boy added a zero (0) to the hundred written on the one hundred dollar bill to make it a thousand dollars. They were arrested.

A schoolmate told them they were not smart because there are no such notes as two hundred dollar notes or thousand dollar notes.

He turned to them and say, "Don't lose hope! Next time use a ten dollar note."

ATTRACTIVE

A young fellow paid a compliment to a lady telling her how attractive she was. When she smiled, he asked, "Madam ! Do you have any children?"

She told him she had three.

He stared at her in shock with mouth wide open in disbelief.

She thought from his reaction that she had looked like she did not have any so she turned to him and asked, "What is the matter?"

He should have said nothing.

Instead he opened his big mouth and said, "Are you sure you don't have nine."

She walked away looking so sad.

THUNDER

A loud, clapping sound of thunder always cause the dogs and cats to run from the outside to the inside of my house. My mother would run and close the windows.

One day the dogs and cats began to run from the inside to the outside of the house.

Mother went to close the windows but stopped when I told her the explosion she heard came from my father's rear. My mother shouted, "I hope it didn't tear."

NUMBER

After the first day at school, a parent checked with her four year old as to what she had learned. She said, Mammy I learned that if you want to pass water you must tell the teacher you want to Number 1.

She went on, "If you want to 'stool' you must ask teacher to allow you to go to Number 2.

She started to laugh. She said that ten minutes after the teacher explained all of that to the children in the classroom a little girl did number 3 in the class.

When her mother questioned her as to what was Number 3, she said that the little girl did both 1 and 2 in the class.

TRAVEL

My Trinidadian friend retired from his job at age sixty-five. He had always said he wanted to travel when he retired, before he passed on to the "Great Beyond". Within one week he travelled from Arima to Moruga then he went from Cocorite to Maraval, and from Chaguanas to Port-of-Spain.

These are all towns and villages in his homeland of Trinidad.

INTERVIEW

I dreamt I was interviewing the Prince of Cricket, Brian when I posed this question to him.

"I know you have the most runs in a single innings in both first class and test cricket. Is there any person or persons you ever feared on the cricket field?"

His answer was quick, "Thieving umpires at the wicket."

He went on to say that he had another record that he had a record that people don't know about.

I asked him, "What?"

He told me, "The record for the most thief out."

COLLAPSE

My son was listening to the news. He heard the newscaster mentioned something about collapse.

He shouted, "My Gosh! Not the West Indies cricket team again."

52

CHEATER

A lady cheated on her white husband with a black guy. No one could understand why. When she became pregnant she worried for nine months. At birth she worried no more because the baby was albino.

THOUSAND DOLLAR NOTE

A young man secretly made some thousand dollar American notes to celebrate a Republican victory in the 2007 American elections. He used a picture of George Bush to put on the note. .

He had to abandon the idea because after the result of the elections when the democrats took control of both houses George Bush face changed.

COLOURS

Jack pulled out some notes from his wallet. He noticed that the two dollar, five dollar, ten dollar and fifty dollar notes from all the countries except America were made of different colours.

Stupid Jack then asked an American, "Why are all of your bills the same colour?"

His reply was, "It's just what you think; we're saving on ink."

53

GOOD MORNING

A sixty year old man entered a liquor store (A Rum Shop in Barbados) early one morning and ordered a Rum and Coke.

He did not say good morning so the barman got angry with him.

He stretched and shouted, "I went gambling, lost my house my car and now my wife, so you tell me what is good about the morning."

IMAGINE IT

Daddy decided to take a nap under a coconut tree. He was off to sleep in a few minutes. He got up just as quick because in his face a bird had shit.

His son ran home with this rhyme :-

Mummy, Mummy come quick, quick, quick
On Daddy nose, a bird just shit

PARTY TIME

It is not unusual for a father to introduce his son or daughter to friends using the first three letters of a child's name in our district.

At this party Patsy's dad said, "Meet my Pat."

Nancy's father introduced her by saying, "Meet my Nan."

Instead of Assad's father introduce him differently he embarrassed the boy with, "Meet my A..."

EXTENTION

Sheila loved a telephone so much that hardly anyone in the house got a chance to use it.

Her father kept complaining since she practically lived on the telephone..

She put in another phone.

What her dad didn't know was that the the new phone was just an extention on the same line.

How I knew he did not know?

He kept complaining to me that every time he picks up the phone he is getting a cross line.

OLD AGE

An man of ninety grabbed his walking stick and went to the village store every Monday. There he would buy two packs of studded condoms and go back home. Every was the same story, he would purchase the condoms and return to his house.

One day the cashier asked him if he is still "beating it". She asked him if he is afraid of HIV/Aids or is it because he doesn't want to get her pregnant,

He smiled and said, "You have the thing wrong, I put them on because at night I does drip bit by bit and my wife says the smell she can't take it.

MOMENT SILENCE

At a recent music show the emcee asked the patrons to stand to observe a minute silence. This was in honour of fallen comrades Kitchener and Ras Shorty I for their cotribution to music. The auditorium went still and silent. You could hear a pin drop.

Everyone burst out laughing when the emcee, broke the moment's silence by inadvertently letting off what was describe as an explosion coming from his rear. (a fart)

QUITE EASY

Some cadets were given a map of the world and asked to find Turkey. They looked and they looked and just could not find Turkey. Suddenly a child shouted, "I find it! I find it!"

All of them turned to him asking , "How did you find it?"

He turned to them saying, "I looked for Greece because a turkey does be in grease!"

56

FINGER

AIDS cases were on the rise so officials were sent into districts to educate and get persons to be tested for HIV/AIDS.

One lady when approached rejected the offer saying that she was sure she did not have the disease and was absolutely certain that she would not catch it.

She said that for her to catch the deadly disease some one would have to cut off her index finger.

She said she does suck on it (her finger) whenever she feels to make love.

SPEAKER

Marcia never said good morning or good evening to anyone. She was a stuck up kind of person who would hardly speak to anyone.

Everyone thought it strange when one morning they saw her speaking to everyone she met. She even said good morning to a known deaf guy standing outside his gate.

It was quite puzzling.

It was only after reading the newspaper that people realised that the newly formed government had made her Speaker.

MET OFFICE

The forecaster predicted that there would be heavy showers in Barbados, St. Lucia and St.Vincent.

Everyone took precautions, only to realise that the there was not a drop of rainfall in any of these countries.

The forecaster was correct however because there was actual flooding in Barbados, St. Lucia and St.Vincent, some streets in Federation Park of Trinidad.

SHORTLY

---- shortly ---

Johnny is the class clown. One day the teacher gave the children some clock faces. She asked them to put in the clock hands and write the time shown under each clock.

Johnny drew two short hands and wrote shortly under his clock face.

He told the teacher that whenever he asked his dad what time he would be back he would always say, "Shortly."

58

FLOODING

Early one Saturday morning Marcus turned up at the vet's office without a pet.

The vet asked him, "How can I help you Sir?"

Marcus began to take off all of his clothes and told the doctor that he would pay her any amount of money of she could get his **dog** to bark.

SWEETHEART

Susan and Ken were lovers for more than two years.

Ken was and old man with lots of money who gave Susan what ever she wanted.

One day Susan asked Ken for his photograph. She wanted to show him to her friends when they got together.

Two nights later she went out with her girlfriends. They were chatting about their boyfriends. They took out pictures of their partners and each boasted that their fellow was the most handsome.

Susan took out her picture and showed them.

They burst out laughing asking if that was really her sweetheart. They said he was old and not too cute.

Her response was , "He might not be cute but he has the loot."

DENTIST

The first time my grandfather went to get a tooth extracted he was in tatters. I never knew he was so afraid of the dentist.

He sat in the waiting area. The dentist came to the door saying, " Next!"

My grand-dad started screaming, "I don't like the dentist!"

Misunderstanding what he meant by I don't like the dentist, the dentist in anger, pulled out the wrong tooth.

FLIES

A Guyanese man came to visit us. He explained that life was hard in his country so he decided to come and live with us here in Barbados.

To survive he said he was cutting down trees and was charging one hundred dollars an hour.

We got him to cut down some trees for us. The job took him four hours.

We paid him four hundred Guyanese dollars and he got angry.

My dad explained to him that he was of the opinion, he was expecting payment in his Guyranian currency.

He felt so bad, all he could say was, "That explains the bad is in Bar*bad*os?"

N.B:- *One thousand Guyranian dollars is equivalent to approximately one US dollar.*

EXOTIC BIRDS

When Marcia went to visit Maria her friend, she showed her an exotic bird. Her husband had given it to her for her birthday.

The bird was so pretty that Marcia went home and told her husband, she wanted an exotic bird for her fifth wedding anniversary.

Lying next to him the morning of their anniversary, after making love all night, she asked him, "Did you get me my bird?"

He turned to her saying, "Sweetheart there is no bird more exotic than mine"

ANNIVERSARY

At a recent church service the priest called on all persons celebrating birthdays to raise their hands. He then called on them to raise their hands if they were celebrating an anniversary such as a wedding, a graduation and so on.

He thought he had finished when an very old man said he was celebrating a special anniversary.

He had the priest puzzled when he said, "I am celebrating five years of death."

Seeing he was alive and kicking the congregation started laughing.

It was then he said, "Yes I am alive and well but a part of me is dead as hell."

OBSERVATION

When James Brown died, the tabloids and some newspapers were quick to highlight things negatives about him.

After first criticizing they wouuld then go on to make mention of the positives about him.

Their stories spoke of him being a woman beater and of his imprisonment first after which they mention his contribution to music.

My son turned to me and asked, "Why do our people always have to highlight things negative before the positive?"

I said to him that if you look at the plus sign (+) commonly referred to as the positive sign, people always write the negative (-) part of the sign before adding the vertical or upright stroke.

He asked of me, "Dad,! Is that the reason why Bajans booed you when you performed for them at the Sir Garfield Sobers Auditorium?"

All I could say was, "Son! To be accepted among your own it seem like you must first be rejected.

He understood as I went on to mention other local performers like Rhiana who came under the hammer for an outfit she wore on her return to her homeland. To me it was punishment for her sudden and quick rise to being a superstar.

Tribute To Sa Luche

This year a comrade, friend and fellow comedian from the island of St. Vincent passed on.

Sa Luche and I performed in Trinidad. Before I went on stage he sat me down and told me of what I should and should not say in the Land of the Humming Bird.

He said, "Never make a joke on a Trinidadian during your performance." This he thought would be a recipe for boos.

He proceed to tell me of a Trini joke he wanted to tell but knew he couldn't tell it in Trinidad.

In his memory I take this opportunity to tell it for him.

After Lara had made two ducks in a Test Match in Trinidad, **Sa Luche** told me that Chanderpaul and Lara had gone into a restaurant to buy dinner.

He said the queue was long so Lara went to the bathroom leaving Chanderpaul to make the order.

On his return Lara asked Chanderpaul what he had ordered.

Shiv told him he had ordered two chicken rotis for himself.

Lara then asked, "And what for me?"

He said, "Two ducks."

Sa Luche you are sadly missed.

More laughs and
more poetry

Now you can also collect these
family favourites....